PRAYERS FROM THE WILDERNESS

Prayers
from the
Wilderness

M. Richardson

Old Sea
PUBLISHING

Photography & design by M. Richardson.

ISBN-13:
Hardcover 979-8-9989838-0-1
Paperback 979-8-9989838-1-8
Ebook 979-8-9989838-2-5

First Edition

Published by Old Sea Publishing
oldseapublishing.com

To all the seekers, doubters, and dreamers:
ask—keep asking,
seek—keep seeking,
knock—keep knocking.

Table of Contents

Preface

This is a book from the field. It is not a statement about the life of faith, but a demonstration of what that sometimes looks like. It is honest.

Written over more than 30 years, it follows the ups and downs of joys, difficulties, doubts, and hopes. Each chapter represents a different part of the journey.

A river flows from one point to another, but along the way there are shallows, rapids, and eddies. Likewise our path has a start and end, but the days inside it contain cycles and undulations. As sure as every mountaintop is followed by a valley, in the darkness of the valley we know that we will one day see a mountaintop again.

Throughout all these changes, one thing is constant: God is there with us. Even when we can't see Him. Even when we don't feel it. He is even more faithful than the steady rising of the sun, day after day after day.

No matter where your journey takes you, I hope you find some comfort or encouragement in these pages. Keep walking, keep praying, keep chasing after God with an honest and open heart. And know that you are not alone.

How precious also are your thoughts to me, O God!
How vast is the sum of them!
If I were to count them, they would be more in number
than the sand. (Psalm 139:17–18)

Setting Out

(leaves)

when the moon is
too distant
the sand and stars
too numerous
for this little mind
to comprehend

when the vastness
of the universe
numbs and blinds me
to the things
i should understand

it's in the trembling
of a few sparse leaves
on an autumn-stained tree
that who You are
begins to be
revealed to me.

(here am i)

here am i, dear One
here am i
waiting to become
the one You've called

oh beautiful eyes
looking through the lens
of a work complete

oh skillful hands
shaping the clay
into all they foresee

here am i, dear One
here am i
resting my hope
on Your mastery

arms open wide
singing here am i
the harvest awaits
send me.

(calling)

the flame kept glowing
and the bush kept burning
        but it was not consumed

and moses said, but who am i?
and God said, this will be your sign—

after you step out
after you overcome
        many doubts and dangers

after you go back to the land
that put a price on your head

after you convince all the people
who rejected and ridiculed you
        to follow you

after you face the king
who wants to destroy you
        over and over again

and witness great and terrible things—
blood for water
        pests and pestilence
                plague, destruction, darkness

after the angel of death passes over
and all midnight turns to tears

after you flee
with your bread on your shoulders
        still resting in the bowl

and face the barren wilderness
under the shadow of a tower
        of cloud and fire

after the enemy pursues you to the brink
and you stand trapped
on the edge of the sea

after its waters pile up in a heap
leaving dry land for your feet

after the same waters
consume your enemies
        after you sing for joy

you will suffer thirst
        but I'll make the water sweet
and you'll suffer hunger
        but I'll rain down bread to eat

you'll draw life from dead rocks
and with many wonders
        I will prove you

after all this, all the people you led
will hate you
        and turn their backs
                and shame you

then I will bring you back to this mountain
and you will serve Me

then, and only then, will you know
        that I have sent you.

(not of it)

in it
but not of it
and how we need
to love it
with a hatred
so pure
the disease
meets its cure
and all those
below
rise above it.

(unbelief)

when i look up the road
i see a great question mark
looming pitch-black on the horizon
with dark clouds magnetized
to its stoic sides

when You look up the road
You see a great exclamation point
shimmering with splashes of color
luminescent, glittering inside
full of bright surprise

oh help me to trust Your vision
to hope for what i still can't see
and when my faith goes dark
let this plea bring relief:

Lord i believe,
help my unbelief.

(fool)

i'll be the fool
if that's what You want me to be,
though the solemn-faced
look on with pity,
though the know-betters
and good-intentioned
only see the hurt,
the vanity

hanging on isn't easy—
You never said it would be—
but i know You're crafting
a greater story;
so whatever my role
i'll play it with gladness,
only teach me the difference
between faith and madness

and when all my counselors
eye with contempt
the steps they can't perceive,
let me still be content
to follow Your lead,
trusting You to meet
every silent need.

(exodus)

the things we've seen
will not quickly leave us—
blood and plagues and darkness for days

when the destroyer passed over
we heard the cry of midnight sorrow
and felt its hand upon our throats
cruel and incomprehensible

they have treated us with contempt
abused and despised us
for nearly half a thousand years
but today in our eyes
they are mothers bereft of children
brothers left alone

we sought out treasure
each one from her neighbor
now we gather the plunder
a mere token for our labors

the earth heaves forth one last time
and pushes us out into the desert
the unknown stretches before us
but we are all together
conquerors, fugitives
marching under the banner
of a God of cloud and fire

what lies ahead are wonders we can't foresee
but as we step into the wilderness
we know one thing:
today at last, we are free.

Under the Stars

(the promise)

look up to the sky
where beauty resides
a thousand jewels
spread glimmering white
embodying joy
love and adventure
a story in every
stellar picture

now miles may come
and people may go
but the eyes of strength
run to and fro
and in this luminous
promise we see
wherever the moment
or season may lead

the same sky encircles
you and me.

(vapor)

we are clouds in the sky

        just floating by

                for a little while.

(northern star)

You are my northern star—
i'll follow wherever You lead
near or far, clear to the edge
of the boundless sea

no dying nor living
nor leaving is too hard
every mile finds its worth
the beauty, the scars

the sky circles 'round You,
a dance for the divine
whole worlds lose their way
in the train of Your light

oh heart of my heart
my will and might
this tattered sail presses
through the darkest night

longing just to be where You are—
my northern star.

(instrument)

so far below God
so far above me
and when i get to partake
i'm amazed

a conduit to heaven
a language for the stars
a word that speaks softly
to the needful heart
a voice for the prophets
an instrument of praise

and who are we
who am i
to be granted to taste

grace
infinite grace.

(a boat & a handful)

a boat and a handful
and a twinkle in the eye
a handful of stars
a handful of stars

the sea with its waves
even good sense defies
for a handful of stars
a handful of stars

hold fast, arm of grace
ever true to provide
a handful of stars
a handful of stars

and as You make way
bring a boat and a light
and a handful of stars
a handful of stars.

(here & now)

what if there's more to life
than the end game
the bright everlasting

what if there's a today
in itself
worth the day-to-day

what if there's a purpose
even beyond the great beyond

where simply being a living being
has a magnitude all its own

what if beauty is a calling
for the sake of beauty itself
and laughter and hope
and love

what if our work
is less transparent than it seems

what if there's value
in the dreaming
not merely in the dream

when we look up
watching, waiting
let us not forget to look around

for thanksgiving
shines its brightest
in the humble here and now.

(madding midnight)

the night falls dark
without horizon
and weight on the soul
from every direction

the finish line seems
so far away
hope sacrificed
to distortion—
what small potential,
how meager my portion

but here is grace for tired eyes
and every broken back:

eventually this madding midnight
will fade into the black
and in its place—
oh morning!

what does my Maker
now say to me
but that You've heard
every word
and yet unspoken plea

my treasure
my exceedingly great reward
i will choose this day to fear
to put on a garment
of thanks and praise

for You are the God
who hears.

(naïve)

how many years
behind that youthful smile?

how many tears
behind that lucid thought?

how many fears
behind that confident word?

what has time given you
that i haven't got?

(sufficient)

sufficient for every need
that's what You are to me
able to hold these feet secure
on the crest of the stormy sea

breath in the midst of sails
the wind whose will prevails
my starting point and destination
and hope that never fails

starlight to show the way
peace that can't be explained
a promise of morning light
strength that will never wane

sufficient for every need
that's what You are to me
able and earnest to complete
what You've begun so beautifully.

(intercession)

these groanings can't be uttered
this care won't come undone
their meaning clothed in mystery
some hidden race they run

the Spirit makes intercession
and what would be today
if not for this silent space—
breath between breath
thought between thought—
somewhere in a secret place

how deep the soul is stirred
love's full manifestation
with words it can't discern
the unspeakable conversation.

By the Sea

(red sea)

hot on the heels
thunder, hooves and wheels
the old world
tries to apprehend me

nowhere in sight
to run left or right
and ahead
an unyielding sea

no time to waste
the sun in its haste
petitions
to conclude the day

so i eke out a whisper
so soft to my Maker
won't You please
make for me a way.

(kite strings)

kite strings—
we hold a thin line
on life
and hopes
and dreams

we reel it in
and let it out
and tug
and spin around
as visions dance
before our eyes

but skilled as
we may be
at hanging on
tightly
to those strings
and letting go
at just the right time

we are ever dependent
on that unseen
unsearchable
ever-present
untamable
force of wind—
the breath that keeps us
in the sky.

(bottle)

will You keep this one too?
a lonely drop
suspended in time

a secret prayer
uttered in silence
as moonlight dances
on the water

You write them all
and keep them close—

in Your book a tale
of lost todays
and brave tomorrows

in Your bottle
an ocean of sorrows.

(enough)

i know You
let that be enough
when the sky turns dark
and the sea grows rough

i trust You
let that be enough
when the way is grim
and the going's tough

i'm leaning
on unfailing love
when it's all i've got
let that be enough.

(lighthouse)

somehow the ship
has been blown off course
i need a lighthouse

i can see the wreckage
of those who came before
i need a lighthouse

a steady guide to help
make sense of the night
a beacon unshaken
by the howling storm

ahead appear hazards
and shores unexplored
i need a lighthouse.

(the tide)

sorrow
deep as an ocean
joy
unspeakable

sorrow
deep as an ocean
joy
unspeakable

the weight presses
without, within
the light blooms and dims

the tide goes out
the tide comes in
and goes back out again.

(quiet desperation)

the sky hangs luminous
lavish
in an oversized golden frame

like a child refusing sleep
the day will not go quietly
not till someone listens
to what it has to say

gravity

there's been too much
on too many shoulders
the fabric is about to break

trust is hard to come by
out of the shadows
they creep rank and file
behind the guardians of hate

and no one here knows
how long it's gonna take

so we try to remember
the good old days
the parts worth taking away

but the past is still
too close for comfort
every day we're living
every one of our mistakes

it's nearly suffocating

but for a moment
before the dark

as the sun sweeps down
in slow motion
unashamed of its fiery wings
You invite us
to forget all these things

to take a break from grieving
the melancholy of evening
to revel in beauty
spectacular beauty

and remember to trust
there's a bigger dream

oh we need You
desperately
and we don't know
what that means.

(33)

don't know where to start
but there's nothing going on
but there's
so
much
going
on
eddies all around
new vistas unfolding
and Your love is
strong.

(waiting)

i look for You by the sea
what is it You want
to say to me

my pen is ready
my heart undone

waiting for my only One

i hear Your whisper
in the morning waves

clouds give way
to an early embrace

a breath of salt
a deep blue peace

together we start the day.

(fury)

My love is a stormy sea
and you, a ship on its waves

I will surround you
I will move you
I will set you free

I am a wild, wild sea
and you, the object of My fury

jealous for you
I will cover you
I will swell with rage

and the fierceness of My breath
will save.

(walk by faith)

nowhere to turn, nowhere to hide
enemies gaining from behind
no way across, no way to reach the other side

looking ahead, caught on the edge
can't find another way to go
hands in the air, lift up a prayer and watch the show

> see them rise
> waters like a wall before your eyes
> take your stand
> you're gonna cross on dry land

> but you've gotta walk by faith

no giving in, can't let them win
freedom awaits, be not afraid
too long in chains, this is your chance to break away

pillar of cloud, pillar of fire
shade in the desert, guiding light
with God at your side, nothing's impossible tonight

> the sea will rise
> waters like a wall before your eyes
> take your stand
> you're gonna cross on dry land

> but you've gotta walk by faith.

On the Mountain

(elijah & the sleeping tree)

in the wilderness i lay
under a broom tree
unable to understand
all that had become of me

the plan seemed in place
signs and wonders for days
till i found on my head
a price i couldn't pay

and what was it all for?
a grand story turned to ash
was i really no better
than the failures of the past?

i prayed the good Lord
would end my misery
for who will remember
a broken legacy?

but out in the wilderness
under my sleeping tree
a messenger came to me
saying:

> here is bread for your journey
> and water for your soul
> the road is too long
> yes, take it all

in the wilderness i sat
under a broom tree
watching the horizon
stretch out endlessly

i saw a plan
so much bigger than me
and my strength so very small

so i took the water
and bread from the coals
twice he urged me
so i took it all

then i summoned my courage
found my feet
and set my face
toward the mountain.

(summit)

one breath, one step
one day at a time
taking on a mountain
making it mine

a race not for speed
nor a battle for strength
the peak conquered only
by patience and faith

now souls rest on high
and dreams dwell in clouds
but mortals must fight
on the merciless ground

one breath, one step
one more weary night
till at last that summit
comes into sight.

(sierra)

i want to be in these mountains
when the rocks cry out
when the trees begin to shout Your name

i want to hear their echoes off granite peaks
as the valley turns to flame

wildflowers blossom like a wildfire
light pours down like a waterfall
the mountains tremble and shake

one day we will be restored
and all Your works will sing Your praise.

(the brazen also)

let You be my romance
my song the consequence
how could i be so brazen
to wish beyond the best

let You be my all in all
a melody to fill the heart
be my source, my lovely end
my pure and ultimate art

but what's this little voice inside
that claims it's not too brash
to hold the other desires as well
at least enough to ask

let You be my romance
my joy to never stop
and light this life with hope to hope
even for a cherry on top.

(YHWH yireh)

in the mount of the Lord
it shall be provided

> when all has gone dark
> and you've come to the end

>> when the promise
>> is as good as dead

so bind your living sacrifice
and reach for the knife

on the third day you'll receive him
back to life.

(zacharias, before the angel shows up)

see the multitude standing before You
waiting
waiting

the lot fell to me
my brothers look on
my uncles, their sons

i look back at the people
their eyes burn like the flame in my hand

the weight of hope looms low
fear of disappointment
weariness

faces watch expectantly
heads down, arms raised
some crumbled to their knees

i walk in

it's my turn
to take the fire to the altar
to watch the smoke rise to heaven
vanishing as quick
as a prayer barely spoken

who am i to stand here
the tide of ten thousand stifled breaths
as eager to push me in
as to pull me back out again

courage
selflessness
will i find them?

will the moment steal into my heart
before it so slowly
so quickly ends?

i reach out to light the incense
steadying a hand so heavy
it nearly takes my breath away

the prayers of all these people
the hope, the ache
things too hard to say

this moment defies me to speak my own—
i stopped asking long ago
though i feel it just the same

i push back the pain and simply say,
"God have mercy,
grant the prayers of each and every one"

and for me . . . a son.

(still small voice)

and after the fire
a still small voice
up till now it was almost
predictable

> i ran to the mountain and hid in the rock
> i said this must be my end of days

the wind could not move me
though the mountains
fell to pieces

for what is yet one more enemy

the earth could not shake me
my hands already
so used to trembling

nor was i scorched by the flame

> i ran to the mountain and hid in the rock
> i said this must be my end of days

but when i heard Your voice
i was stirred
the stillness left me shaken
my soul began to burn

i wrapped my face
and slowly came near

here was something new—
no more flight, no more fear

i ran to the mountain and hid in the rock
i said this must be my end of days

but now i know You—even You
are here by my side

and seven thousand beside.

(stones & sling)

what is there in my hand
but a few small stones and a sling
of little consequence are these things
when i have You

i tried to take up the sword
the armor of a king
they were too heavy for me
but i don't need them

> for we are not saved by spear or sword
> no, the battle is Yours

how many nights have grown dark
hunters, thieves on the prowl
every one would have devoured me
but i don't fear them

and when ghastly giants shout
words of terror, indignation
i will not shrink back, turn aside
or entertain them

> for we are not saved by spear or sword
> no, the battle is Yours

see here in my hand
just a few small stones and a sling
but all this is nothing to me
when i have You.

(mountain & valley)

down in the valley
is where the water flows
down in the valley
where the fruit trees grow
up on the mountain
a strong wind blows
and bright the daystar glows

up on the mountain
all heads are bowed
up on the mountain
their songs ring out
down in the valley
a cry comes aloud
from the lips of a madding crowd

down in the valley
the heights are a blur
down in the valley
they fumble for words
up on the mountain
belief procures
a promise that long endures

up on the mountain
hope still abides
up on the mountain
glory resides
but down in the valley
where dreams go to die
is where the harvest lies.

In the Valley

(down in the valley)

down in the valley, it's hard to see beyond the clouds that
obscure the top of the mountain. and it's too easy to
forget i was just there. i was just there. the world
spread out before me and i saw so many roads.
some went winding, winding. some were
perfect lines. i laid out a map in my
mind, all so clear, next steps and
things to believe in. i took
courage in the light that
blanketed the horizon,
the little peaks and
rivers down below.
i almost knew
where to
go.
i followed
the trail down
the mountainside
with all my ideas in
tow, but as i descended
the little hills grew higher,
the golden valley grew
dark beneath the
sinking sun's
glow.

by the time i reached the bottom,
i couldn't find my road.

(gargoyles)

can You really make it all new
when the years feel like a loss
when the best of times
bring the deepest sadness

can You heal

can we remember without tears
what once was so real
can You put a joy in us
that the past cannot steal

forward, onward
one foot follows the other
one day we look back
and don't recognize
what's become of our lives

what of the lightness
that painted the season
what of the purity, ignorance even

building, building
all these years
i thought it was something beautiful

but when i step back all i see
are gargoyles.

(designed to fly)

where's the sun that used to shine
the light that lived behind these eyes
spring approaches, days grow dark
hope forsakes the weary heart

trapped in a body born for defeat
destiny lingers just out of reach
but i still remember how it felt
to be alive, and even well

oh when will You at last revive
and give me wings designed to fly
or am i a fool to hold so tight
that what You offered was the sky?

(prayer for a broken heart)

need
want
try
confusion

hope
love
lose
delusion

break
mend
calm
the madness

help
please
take
the sadness.

(abraham comes near to the Lord)

the angels walk on
but i wait with You;
the things in my heart
would be foolish to air
so instinctively, like a child,
i come near—
as if all reality doesn't rest
in the palm of Your hand,
my destiny in what You answer me

i feel the space, the time
the silence around us;
a lone cricket chirps
from the dry grass;
the grass stirs as a
breeze edges past
causing the oaks to whisper
with a soft grandeur,
the afternoon a symphony

suddenly the rustle
of the tent door behind me
reminds me i'm an intruder here—
a mortal, a lump of clay
standing dangerously close
to heaven's door;
yet something in Your eyes,
the slant of Your shoulders
invites me to stay

so, like a fool
i draw in a breath
and summon the courage
for what i want to say;

maybe i should be afraid
but in the stillness—
the sunlight in Your face
the way You never turn away—
i know i am safe.

(sunrise over sodom)

I gave you the night
and so many before
you had your choices
you chose the storm

I gave you the night
and so many before
when fire rains down
don't say you weren't warned

I made a way out
and offered My hand
but a time must come
to close the door

so I give you this night
like so many before
but when the sun rises
that time will be yours.

(shadows)

Lord, i'm walking through the valley again
shadows are growing long again
just when i think i've reached the end
i hear them roar again

how much longer?

Lord, i need to hear Your voice again
to feel Your living strength again
to see You outshine the darkness
and give me hope again

how much farther?

Lord, i need to hear You sing again
it's not a sentiment
i need You to walk with me, carry me
lift me up on eagle's wings

how much longer?

(refiner's fire)

so long in the refiner's fire
years and months and days and counting

heat builds as the flame grows higher
caught in the blaze, pressure mounting

the Lord gives
and takes away

so long in the refiner's fire
courage melts, hope almost ceasing

but somewhere in the midst of the pyre
is a glimmer, a spark of faith increasing

the Lord works
in mysterious ways.

(morning promise)

You have every idea
what this means to me—
a morning promise
and hope

after a little while
and things i don't really
want to talk about
You'll still be around

to complete the dream
fulfill the agony
and put life and strength
back into me.

Through the Desert

(souls in prison)

souls in prison
for profits
not their own
laboring to build
a life
they'll never know
paying off debts
never acquired
puppets emptied
upon evil desire
lured with promises
captured by deceit
held by force
no haven to retreat
washed by the needle
chained by the gun
bodies unable
to simply run
and far too many
far too young
to know their right
to know right
sold by loved ones
strangled
by satan's appetite
oh won't You rescue
these millions alive
shelter them
in Your healing light
and put the darkness
to flight.

(meditation on zechariah)

can't we just skip to the ending
past the parts unspeakable
to the flowing river and light undimmed

can't we just hear Your voice
and fly up to meet You
and leave all the rest of it to the wind

they'll run to the mountain
to find the way You made
You'll hide them in a safe place

and all the people will mourn
and all the earth will shake
and one bright day, we'll see Your face

just a little longer—
a long and terrible longer—
but even in the dark, You're not so far away.

(Jesus in the desert)

i wish i could have walked with You
the same dust kicked up on our feet
and watched the miles melt into hours
just You, me, and the desert heat

i wish i could have heard Your thoughts
when no one was around to listen
and felt Your silence and weary breath
brought on by the ache of distance

i wish i could have seen Your eyes
from the side as they searched the horizon
the infinite fire of a Master's gaze
sunburnt, longing for mountains.

(holes & nests)

foxes have holes
and birds have nests
but tonight these eyes
will find no rest

wandering, waiting
for the coveted day
when my head at last
has somewhere to lay

i'm tired, so tired
of not knowing when
this lonely road
will come to an end

a city of strangers
nowhere a friend
and yet every lion
retires to a den.

(faith)

faith is a
long-distance love
dressed up and waiting
endlessly
anticipating

not so mindful
of the joy to come
as of the arduous
day at hand

it's the ache
of past and future
culminating
in the unknown
of each moment
undefinable

it's patience
wearing a tired
morning face
as she wonders
how much longer
how much longer?

(wandering ewe)

have You brought me out
into the desert
to kill me?

stop my wicked mouth

the miraculous unfolds
before my eyes
yet in my heart

grows a garden of doubt

what a horrid condition
that one so delivered
could question love

as it rains down help

forgive all my weaknesses
callous and blind
be my guide

and save me from myself.

(still here)

they threw out the book
now you have no truth to turn to
in a war of words and ideologies

the gatekeepers turn away
there's no one left to defend you

but I'm still here

when the darkness creeps
when all you see are shadows
all you've gotta do is turn around

'cause I'm still here

I am the light that never wanes
I am the truth, I never change
I am the life they can't take away
when you're lost, I am the way

they'll batter you with doubt
and beat you with their waves
but there is a Rock high and safe

and I'm still here.

(stone & lily)

i gave You my youth
but it was nothing
i fell down like a battered wall
crumbled, forsaken

but You would not leave me

i gave You what i could
but it was nothing
i withered like a winter bloom
hungry for sun

but You sustained me

You gave me all of You
when i had nothing

and one day
when the morning comes
i'll rise with the living

i'll be a stone with eagle wings
clothed like a lily in spring
i'll be a stone with eagle wings
clothed like a lily in spring

and these weathered old bones
will sing.

(unloved—malachi's burden)

I have loved you

yet all day long you gnash your teeth
and make up accusations against Me

I gave you life
I gave you everything
I gave you life
you threw it back at Me

I made the sun shine down
you ran for cover
I put food on your table
you offered it to another

I put clothes on your back
you turned your back on Me
I promised you peace
you dealt treacherously

your words are harsh

all day long you gnash your teeth
and make up accusations against Me

I gave you wisdom
you refused to listen
I gave you mercy
you threw it back at Me

you've stolen what was Mine
and won't pay what you owe
you corrupt My words
and won't do what you're told

you've sold the needy
turned away the stranger
and you treat with contempt
our time together

I gave you life
I gave you everything
I gave you life
you threw it back at Me

if all that weren't enough
now you tell Me you're the one
who's unloved.

At the Cross

(back to the garden)

here in the eve
we stroll across the brook
back to the garden we know
we've come here before
but tonight it's different

i don't comprehend all Your words
but i feel their weight
like the sky falling down around me

You ask us to watch and wait—it's late
our bones are weary from sorrow
none of us is able to imagine
just what will come tomorrow

tightly we have held You
in heart and hand
though somehow i feel
we still don't understand
just what or who You are

there's a hush in the sky
as though all heaven would sigh
i don't know why, but it takes me

now my eyes grow heavy
my soul perplexed
and not without some fear
in a solemn hour
when strength becomes weak
all heads bow down to sleep—

but i could swear off in the distance
i heard somebody weeping.

(alone)

in the garden again
the place where we first met
together tonight
but somehow

I am alone

sleepers unaware
what lies just over the crest
heavy steps and lungs
swords and clubs

like a thief they come
to take Me away
though I never hid
from the light of day

but My time has come
and now I succumb
with tears and blood
to water your garden

all alone.

(rooster)

the rooster has crowed
this whole thing is dragging on
so long
don't they know He's done
nothing wrong?
they're shouting, laughing
the latter the greater rage

tell me where now
are the blind, the lame?
we are too scared to testify
and not allowed to fight
so we wait

where have they taken Him now
and who owns the hands
that pressed the thorns
into His brow?

it appears our kingdom
was only made of clay
and yet something inside me
believes just the same

here He comes!
our King in a crown
but what's this burden
laid on His back?

He who made bodies whole
stumbling under the weight
He who gave light and hope
head hung in shame

i want to follow close behind
to run up to His side
but i am afraid

my Hero is defeated
put on public display

yet after the tree is raised
He gazes upward and says,
"Father, forgive them."

(mother mary)

i remember those fingers
before they knew how to move
when they first learned
how to grasp and count

i remember those eyes
the first time they looked up
not like today
no, they were full of wonder

monsters tear and thrash
at His broken skin
but in my mind it's still
perfect as the day it was new

a trickle of blood makes its way
down His ankle
and rolls off His big toe
pooling on the ground below

i remember those feet
when they learned how to stand
teetering
with joyful persistence

and now how they shake
as He pulls Himself up straight
to tell me
there's a new son who needs me

but i will not forget.

(from here)

numbness.
as the dawn comes flooding in
it carries the memory
of things i wanted to believe
become nightmares;
it begins with a shadow
writhing behind the eyes
a form emerging in my mind;
i'm reminded of the sound
of hammer and nail
the mocking, jeering, weeping

sickness.
how i wish to return
to sleep and denial
to pretend this new reality
was just a bad dream
but i can still smell the blood, the sweat
and hear the world outside
feebly searching for normal
behind the despair

darkness.
we thought this light
would shine on forever
but it has been extinguished;
i wish i had asked, listened
taken more time
or could somehow bring Him back;
didn't we all believe
salvation had finally come,
now in a flash it's gone—
and where do we go from here?

(emmaus)

yesterday the sky grew black
crushing like a heart attack
if i can barely breathe i'm not alone

cursing mouths and violent hands
brought to bear upon the Man
who held the only dream i'd ever owned

      the only light i'd ever known

turned my back on life and home
ready for a change to come
made myself a fool for prophecy

miracles and broken bread
seeing blind and walking dead
multitudes like rivers in the street

      waving branches for the King

now there's no sense in what i've seen
the hope of nations on a tree
decorated in a thorny crown

blood and water intertwined
running down the mountainside
darkness like an ocean in the clouds

      raining down upon the crowd

friday night i had a dream
the world was crashing down on me
saturday i woke to find it real

ruin in the house of peace
a city cast upon its knees
confusion in the lines on every face

and sunday only promises the same—

friday night i had a dream
the world was crashing down on me
saturday i woke to find it real

empty hands believe no more
this isn't what you bargained for
bought a kingdom, all you got was shame!

so take your coat
            put on your shoes and go
                    away from here
                            it's time to face your fear

and make the long walk home.

(only Son)

who carved these marks into Your hands?
who drew these scars across Your brow?
when i look at You
i see the end of every desire
the means i've been missing

but somewhere i lost my way

i waited lifetimes for You to come
what kind of nightmare turned
the prints of my hands to blood
captivated by an unknown suitor
confused, desperate, led astray

sold to the lowest bidder

oh Beloved!
my heart fails to fathom
just what i have done
wake me up
let this all vanish away
hide my eyes from what i've become

for in cold blood
with curses on my tongue

i have betrayed my only Son.

(the river)

You are the river
the way we cross over
from the struggle
to the promised land

You are the hope
that waits with arms open
and calls us
to put our feet in

You are the bridge
that forms when the water
shrinks back from
the touch of Your hand

You are the river
that cleanses the broken
to bring us to life
once again.

Coming Home

(the morning that broke time)

a breath of blue greets the horizon,
the third day of our sorrows.

careful not to wake anyone
we leave our beds, soaked with tears,
gather our things
and steal into the dark
of the waiting morning.

heavy hearted,
we do what we must do.
fear lurks at every corner,
every noise a reason to turn back—
but for the birds.

singing!

on a morning like this.
a rose glow crests the hilltop;
peace follows like a gentle breeze.
shapes and shadows lead to the garden
where we find the cursed tomb.

silence.

the earth trembles.
strangers greet us
with even stranger news.
we turn back, astonished.
then we see Him.

risen!
alive!
victorious!

(this body broken)

if this body is broken
You were broken for me
if this life trickles out
You were poured out for me

and You won't forget
not ever
the price You paid for me

and You'll never leave
never forsake
never lose Your hold
on this needy soul.

(magdalene)

i can't see for the tears
streaming down my face;
in the east the glow is faint
as though a new day
would dare to break,
but i know not why

why does the sun
continue to rise
when we know it'll never
be the same?
no more hope, no change
no reason to shine

i stoop down to see inside
where my Beloved lay
but through bleary eyes
i see nothing—
now even the memory
has been stolen away

a man speaks
somewhere behind me
unaffected it would seem;
i see a form but turn away
to be left alone
with my grief

just then like music
my name He speaks;
my heart leaps
defying all reason—
i know my Shepherd's voice
i hear Him calling me

before i know it
i am at His feet
the tears i knew before
washed away
by tears of joy
astonished belief

and love

now the sun begins to rise
and i know
things will never be the same
for hope has come back to life
and no grave can hold
the One born to shine

alive forever!
and forever
He is mine.

(cast all your cares)

remember
when you were young
how I carried you in My arms

you've come so far since then
built your kingdom
made a name

but somewhere along the way
you forgot where you belong

now you're feeling shot down
like an arrow took a star from the sky
bewildered
by the wildness around you

but My back is stronger
than the mountains
and My face is made of flint

and they have never turned away

you forgot but I remember you
every hour, every day
you don't know but I know you
and I love you anyway

your burden is heavy
you can throw it all on Me
you don't have to do this alone

you're still My child
and I'd die a thousand times
just to bring you home.

(a home)

not a house to mourn in
nor a hall that echoes
alone
would a giver of good things
give a child a stone?

no, but love looks down
condescending
to comfort the needful soul
like an arc upon the hill
His promise shines full

now when the path is hidden
oh heart let it be known
like a joyful mother of children
He will grant the barren
a home.

(upstream)

like salmon pushing upstream
we've been trying to hold on
so long

the young have grown old
the old and those we once loved
now gone

meant for so much more
bodies battered, stripped to the bone
we groan

looking, longing, loving
pressing onward toward the voice
we know

holding fast with stubborn grasp
the dream, the tireless hope
of home.

(no mortar)

broken, chiseled
displaced, dusty
these stones will fit
together perfectly

one holy building
beautiful to behold
bathed in harmony
decked in gold

once they're carried
to the building site
there will be no sound
of hammer or knife

just the raising of a body
that when completed
will stand unshakable
no mortar needed.

(my mansion)

somewhere up there
with the pearly gates
and gold-covered streets
they say there's a mansion
prepared just for me

will it be built with precious stones
and fine-hewn marble bricks
enclosing a fully stocked fridge,
will it have a TV the size of a football field
mounted on the dining room wall?

no, i'm quite convinced my mansion
won't have any walls at all
no doors or windows, not even a roof
for what good is heaven
if you close it all off?

give me a sand dune
on a lazy crystal shore
with a billion twinkling stars above

give me a garden in the sun
where butterflies flit and flutter
where rainbows sing lullabies
and gardenias smell in full color

with a little nook to lay my head
when i get tired—though i won't get tired
and a lot of peace
and maybe even a little solitude

but most of all
just give me You.

(galaxy)

do You ever miss the silence You knew
before all of this?
does it ever seem like some crazy
mixed-up, backward dream?

You said the word and planets sprung to life
out of spinning, swirling vapor
You pulled everything in sight

      lighting up the world with the fire in Your eyes
      breathing on the dust, bringing it to life

when You walked down the road
with mud on your feet and a threadbare coat
did You ever think of all the things
You traded for suffering?

like a shooting star You came down from above
lived and died a man, rose to shine again
and You did it all for love

now the universe rests in the palm of Your hand
and no eye has seen, nor heart has dreamed
the future You have planned

      lighting up the world with the fire in Your eyes
      breathing on the dust, bringing it to life

all Your wonders are a mystery
and Your heart—

Your heart is a galaxy.

(sunset)

what if this were a golden street
brightly my feet to guide
what if a highway wrought by the sun
a flame on the rising tide

what if i had the courage to stand
outstretching my foot to the sea
what if the faith to trust, even dream
the water could buoy me

sometimes i think i've grown too attached
to the so-called solid ground
for this world will fade like the sun's final rays
and soon i'll be heaven bound

what if this were my day to step out
love's golden street to roam
what if the sound of these waves His voice
calling me sweetly home?

Trust in the LORD with all your heart, and lean not on your own understanding;
In all your ways acknowledge Him, and He will direct your paths. (Proverbs 3:5–6)

About the Author

M. Richardson is a musician and songwriter based in Nashville, Tennessee—a long way from the beach. Originally from the sunny shores of California, she's an unabashed product of the Jesus movement. With a faith that has carried her through the best and worst of times and a path that's taken her all over the world, she is well versed in losing and finding her way.

Index

www.ingramcontent.com/pod-product-compliance
Lightning Source LLC
Chambersburg PA
CBHW031433120626
46545CB00006B/2390